I Dreamed

21 Short Plays

by RICHARD URDAHL

Illustrated by Marlowe Urdahl

FORTRESS PRESS
PHILADELPHIA

Library of Congress Catalog Card Number 74–76919

ISBN 0-8006-0159-9

4265B74   Printed in U.S.A.   1-159

Last Night I Dreamed

Maybe you did too. Well, lie down on a couch and tell me your dreams. Better still, lie down on a *biblical* couch and tell me who you *are* in your dreams. Samson? Delilah? Mary? Let yourself go while I try to understand you, or rather understand the Bible through you. Or maybe you are *in* the Bible when you dream from a biblical couch.

I am not sure who is who in the dreams that follow, but somehow, in a crisp way, they help you get in touch with yourself by dreaming you are someone else. Through these twenty-one short plays Richard Urdahl provides a new glimpse of the magic in our dreams—and of the humor that tricks us into being honest with ourselves. His dreams would make Freud faint without quite knowing why.

Freud is not a biblical figure, despite what some people may think. For as Urdahl says, "Long before Freud convinced the Western world of the revelatory character of dreams, the Eastern world had lived with that knowledge for centuries. The biblical peoples certainly knew about dreams, their importance, and their power. They also knew that dreams often needed interpreting and that those individuals who could interpret them were special people.

"Remember Joseph? He parlayed this ability into a seat at Pharaoh's right hand. And he wasn't even a certified pychoanalyst! And he was under forty, yet! This clearly suggests that powers of interpretation were given to youngish layfolk (an ancient truth suggesting that only youngish layfolk and their kindred spirits will know what to do with this book)."

The dreams in this book are just that: dreams. They are not a grand search for meaning or a new way to interpret life. They are, as Urdahl says, "just dreams—confusing, enlarging, distorting, and expanding a variety of concerns." Bits and pieces from the Bible and religion are "highlighted because they—together with dating, career planning, conflicts between the generations, epidermal blemishes, etc.—are the daily fodder upon which dreams feed."

The interpretations given in these dreams are very tentative. They reflect the nondirective school of counseling where, as Urdahl remarks, "the only firm, tangible, absolute thing the counselor brings with him is his pipe."

You are invited to read these dreams for fun . . . sheer enjoyment. But then also act them out as dream-drama—you need only one other player besides yourself. Make them prefaces to a sermon or a sacrament. Invite your pastor, your parents, your teachers, your friends to react. See where they tune in to these dreams. Let them expose themselves through these dreams. Make these dreams the springboard (or should I say couch) from which to get into the stuff of who you are. Turn these dream figures into puppets and then back into people. Or dream your own dreams with other figures like Balaam, or Balaam's ass.

With Urdahl, "whether you read this book or not, I wish you happy dreams."

Norman Habel
Editor of Open Books

Last
Night
I Dreamed

Last Night

Last Night I Dreamed . . .

1. I Was Some Kind of Priest 1
2. I Was in Church 7
3. I Was in a Burning, Fiery Furnace 10
4. I Had Died 13
5. I Was a Very, Very Famous Theologian 16
6. I Was a Pamphylian 20
7. I Was About Twelve Years Old 23
8. I Was an Old, Old Man 25
9. I Was on the Johnny Carson Show 30
10. I Was Awakened by Five Screaming Women 33
11. I Was, of All Things, a Sheep 36
12. I Was Eating with the Pigs 40
13. I Started Homeward 43
14. I Found My Brother and Wished I Hadn't 48
15. I Was God 52
16. I Was Standing Before a Great Body of Water 54
17. I Was Adam 57
18. I Had Been Reading the Bible 60
19. I Was Beguiled by a Sinister Woman 65
20. My Hair Grew Back 68
21. I Was More Powerful Than a Speeding Locomotive 70

Last Night I Dreamed...

1.

. . . I Was Some Kind of Priest

1: The other night I dreamed I was some kind of priest.

2: A priest, eh?

1: I didn't know for sure just which denomination I belonged to, but I did know I was a priest.

2: You were sure on one out of two counts; that's not bad.

1: That's the way I felt. Anyway, as I said, I was a priest.

2: Yes, I got that.

1: I was galloping down some remote country road on a little grey donkey.

1

2: A donkey?

1: I must have been from a rather poor denomination . . . or . . . maybe it was just a sign of my deep humility, I don't know, anyway. . . .

2: Yes, please continue.

1: I had just had lunch . . . this scene was a kind of flashback . . . I had just had lunch in a little crossroads inn with two strangers, the one a kind of pompous big shot, the other, a foreign-looking fellow whom I somehow didn't quite trust.

2: Oh?

1: Well, for one thing, I don't think he said grace before the meal.

2: A sure sign of moral decadence, eh?

1: Well, since he knew I was a priest you'd have thought he'd at least fake it!

2: I suppose so, but nonetheless, the three of you were eating together, right?

1: It was a very small inn, only one table, so what choice was there? And besides, I was a priest, walking around, you know, saying, "Yes, my son . . . no, my son . . . my son this, my son that" . . . so there you are.

2: An occupational hazard, eh?

1: I had a feeling that things weren't quite right . . . and I was right! After lunch the big shot excuses himself, says something about going to the washroom and before you know it he's beat it off down the road, sticking us with his part of the check . . . and after he'd eaten more than the two of us put together!

2: Rather difficult to act priestly after that, eh?

1: Oh, I didn't say anything rough . . . not out loud, at least . . . so we paid the check and I suggested

that we take off after the thief, adding something to
the effect that it was our duty to curb his antisocial
behavior . . . for the sake of the broader commun-
ity . . . or something like that.

2: A thoroughly priestly thought, eh?

1: But this foreigner says, no, he wants to take a
quick nap before continuing his journey and then
adds that just as our sins have been forgiven we
ought to forgive his sins!

2: And that was a nonpriestly thought?

1: Of course not! But, remember, he was just a layman.

2: Oh?

1: Subject to Layman's Folly.

2: Layman's Folly?

1: Literalism!

2: I see.

1: So I jump on my donkey and . . . as I said at the
beginning . . . I was soon galloping down the road.

2: Anxious to fulfill your priestly duties, eh?

1: I suppose so, but, anyway, after about an hour at
a flat-out gallop I turned a sharp corner and about
fifty yards down the road was the big shot, on his
black stallion, very showy, looking down at something lying in the road. I reined to a halt and noticed that the "something" was a person . . . lying
there all beat up, dirty, bloody . . . a terrible sight.

2: I can imagine.

1: The big shot doesn't even get off his horse to see
if the guy's dead! He just spurs the big stallion on
and leaves the poor beggar in the dust.

2: A thoroughgoing rascal, eh?

1: That's putting it mildly! Anyway, I kicked the
old mule thinking to hurry him along to see what

I could do . . . a drink from my canteen, a bandage or two . . . maybe the last rites, assuming I knew them . . . at least I wanted to help the poor soul.

2: Abandoned your chase of the heartless chiseler, eh?

1: Of course! Here was a person who needed immediate help! Even if I weren't a priest I would have stopped! Anyway, wouldn't you know it, the mule was spooked by the sight—they have a real keen sense of danger, you know—and he bolted right by the guy! I tried everything I could do to get him stopped . . . no luck! He ran on for about another hour, with me trying to rein him in all the time, when all of a sudden he stopped and over his head I went! I mean I sailed . . . you-know-what-over-you-know-what!

2: That must have been quite . . . something.

1: After I regained my senses . . . and piety . . . I started limping, hobbling, crawling back toward the poor guy in the road. Oh, yes, the donkey continued on in the opposite direction, never to be seen again. Well, after several hours in the burning, blinding, boiling sun I reached the spot . . . and guess what?

2: You tell me.

1: There was this other guy I had had lunch with, the foreigner, leaning over the victim giving him a drink of water, bandaging his wounds, and lifting him onto one of his two donkeys, the seedier of the two, I might add.

2: Not really such a bad guy after all, eh?

1: Just wait a minute, there's more.

2: I'm not surprised.

1: I came up to this foreigner and asked if there was anything I could do to help. He gave me a dirty look, a very dirty look, and said, no, not a thing! Should I drape my cloak over the poor, naked guy? No, thank you. Should I walk alongside the donkey to make sure the unconscious fellow didn't fall off? Not necessary, he'd tie him on. Could I at least say some sort of prayer? Absolutely not, he might be of a different religion. And would you believe it?

2: What?

1: He just rode off down the rode leaving me standing there!

2: No!

1: And I was in almost as bad shape as the victim!

2: And then?

1: Well, I started walking down the road, hour after hour, on and on, finally, at about midnight I arrived at another inn.

2: And?

1: I staggered in, all but dead, and there was the biggest party going on that you've ever seen!

2: A party, eh?

1: And guess who the guest of honor was?

2: You tell me.

1: You absolutely could not guess!

2: Probably not.

1: THE FOREIGNER!

2: No!

1: Yes!

2: I would never have guessed!

1: Everyone was walking around patting him on the back, buying him drinks, dropping an occasional gold piece in his pocket . . . all because he had . . . get this . . . all because he had shown mercy to the guy on the road, who, it turns out, was a pretty important man in those parts. All that the people could talk about was this wonderful, compassionate foreigner!

2: But you knew differently, eh?

1: You'd better believe it! It made me sick!

2: So?

1: I summoned up what little remaining strength I had and . . .

2: Yes?

1: . . . punched him right smack in the nose!

2: You what?

1: That's right! Right in the nose! Right there!

2: And that was a priestly act?

1: Of course it was!

2: Oh?

1: It was a witness to the Truth!

2: The Truth?

1: That no person is lower than one who hogs a good deed!

2.

. . . I Was in Church

1: The other night I dreamed I was in church.

2: In church?

1: I don't go all that often but I do dream about it quite a bit.

2: Add both experiences together and that just about makes you a member-in-good-standing, doesn't it?

1: I've thought about that, you know, but I doubt that it counts, although it is ironic.

2: Ironic?

1: When I'm not in church I dream that I'm there, but when I am in church I dream that I'm somewhere else.

2: That is ironic.

1: And kind of hilarious. The only way I can get away from church is to go to church!

2: You like to "dream" church but you don't like to "be" church, is that it?

1: It's not that I like it or dislike it, that's just the way it is.

2: Do you think this is a psychological or a theological problem?

1: What?

2: Maybe you should be talking to a theological counselor?

1: What?

2: A clergyman of some kind.

1: Does that mean that you aren't interested in church?

2: That's not what it means.

1: Then what does it mean?

2: That it's not my problem.

1: Does that mean that you do or don't go to church?

2: Neither. It means that your dream, evidently a recurring dream, is troubling you.

1: Oh?

2: So let's talk about your dream, OK?

1: It's my problem, is it?

2: Isn't it?

1: And it's not your problem, right?

2: Right.

1: You're sure?

2: Do you wish it were my problem?

1: May I tell you something?

2: Surely.

1: I think you're being terribly defensive.

2: Oh?

1: Furthermore . . .

2: Yes?

1: Your defensiveness has made this more of a problem than it was originally.

2: I'm to blame, eh?

1: I hadn't thought of it as being either a psychological problem or a theological problem.

2: You hadn't?

1: As a matter of fact, it wasn't even a problem for me.

2: You wanted to talk about it but it wasn't a problem, is that it?

1: I talk about a lot of things that aren't problems for me.

2: Oh?

1: Don't you?

2: You think that counselors are only interested in problems?

1: Not exactly.

2: But you do think that they are more interested in the problems people have than in the people themselves?

1: Well . . .

2: Well?

1: You wouldn't be talking to me if I didn't have a problem, would you?

2: Would you be talking to me if you didn't have a problem?

1: I just told you that I don't have a problem.

2: Then why . . .

1: Am I bothering you?

2: You think you're bothering me?

1: Well, let's just say I have a feeling that if I don't come up with a problem right away you'd wish I'd leave.

2: Well, now, that's the makings for a problem, isn't it?

1: In a way, I suppose.

2: So?

1: OK, so tell me, why do I always fall asleep in church?

2: That's a good question.

1: I'm waiting for a good answer!

2: Now THAT is a problem!

3.

. . . I Was in a Burning, Fiery Furnace

1: Some of my dreams are very ordinary but others are really strange.

2: Seldom predictable, eh?

1: The other night, for example, I dreamed that I was, of all places, in a burning, fiery furnace!

2: A what?

1: I told you that some of my dreams are strange. I was in a burning, fiery furnace!

2: You're right, that's hardly ordinary.

1: For a while I thought I dreamed it because just before I went to bed I ate four pizzas.

2: Four pizzas!

1: I was hungry.

2: Evidently.

1: Four pizzas with the works . . . but heavy on pepperoni and anchovies!

2: And you're still surprised that you had a strange dream?

1: Well, yes. One night I ate five pizzas.

2: And no strange dream?

1: Nope. Of course, come to think of it, I didn't ever fall asleep that night but not because of the pizzas.

2: Oh?

1: Kathy had just given back my class ring!

2: Oh.

1: The night of the Vanilla Fudge concert.

2: Could we get back to the dream . . . the fiery furnace?

1: It was a furnace, all right.

2: And you were in it?

1: I was in it.

2: And?

1: Of course, there was a fire in it! That's what made it so strange.

2: But the fire didn't harm you, eh?

1: That made it pretty strange, don't you think?

2: I should think so.

1: But it, the dream, got even stranger.

2: Oh?

1: There were three other guys in there with me!

2: Oh?

1: And with the strangest names! You wouldn't believe their names!

2: Mr. Pepperoni, Mr. Anchovy . . .

1: Hey! You've never joked about my dreams before!

2: I'm sorry . . . that was most unprofessional. Forgive me!

1: Well, OK, but if this dream is too hot for you to handle I can . . . say, that was pretty good . . . "too hot to handle"!

2: I'm really sorry that I was so gauche. It won't happen again. Please tell me more about your dream.

1: As you rightly guessed, I was surprised (a) because I wasn't being burned alive, (b) because I wasn't alone, and (c) because of what those other guys were doing . . . really weird!

2: Something . . . unnatural, eh?

1: You'd better believe it! They were singing hymns!

2: Hymns?

11

1: Of praise!

2: I see.

1: And thanksgiving!

2: Thanksgiving!

1: Because they weren't being burned alive, I assume.

2: That's fitting.

1: I thought so, so . . .

2: So?

1: I began singing, too!

2: Oh?

1: I'm not what you'd call a true believer, but I sang! Man, did I sing!

2: You knew the hymns?

1: I knew the FEELING!

2: Of thanksgiving.

1: Right, given the circumstances . . .

2: Yes?

1: . . . agnosticism was a luxury I couldn't afford!

2: What happened when you got out of the furnace? You did get out, didn't you?

1: Alive and unsinged!

2: With your new-found faith still intact?

1: Oh, yes. You see, it dawned on me . . .

2: Yes?

1: . . . that in many ways . . .

2: Yes?

1: . . . all of life . . .

2: Yes?

1: . . . is a furnace!

2: So?

1: Sing, baby, sing!

4.

. . . I Had Died

1: The other night I dreamed that I had died.

2: Oh?

1: I read some place that very few people ever dream they actually die.

2: Some parts of the literature do deal with that specific question.

1: But I had died . . . no question about that.

2: I see.

1: What . . . what do they say about people who— you know—who dream they die?

2: It bothered you that you had died?

1: Not in the dream—quite the contrary—but now I'm beginning to wonder.

2: Let's concentrate on the dream, shall we?

1: Trying to weasel out of the question, eh?

2: You still think it's ominous that you dreamed you died?

1: The more you stall around the more ominous it becomes!

2: Would a long dissertation about dreams in general and death in particular have any effect on your dream?

1: I told you it wouldn't.

2: Then why not talk about your dream?

1: You think that I'm really afraid to talk about it?

2: Are you?

1: OK, I'll just show you!

2: Fine.

1: My dream was fine, too! I don't remember dying. I evidently just woke up . . . dead.

2: I see.

1: But I was, I admit, rather surprised.

2: Surprised?

1: Pleasantly surprised . . . overwhelmingly surprised! Believe it or not—frankly, I didn't at the time— the streets WERE golden and all of the houses WERE made of ivory! I was going to say alabaster but I don't know what alabaster is.

2: I see.

1: And this will kill you . . .

2: Yes?

1: People WERE playing harps and there WERE choruses all over the place. Why, even the smallest of them made the Mormon Tabernacle Choir look like a quartet!

2: Really?

1: And everyone—myself included—WAS wearing a shimmering, white robe!

2: Oh?

1: I never dreamed heaven would be like that!

2: Heaven?

1: Well, you don't think . . .

2: Excuse me, I'm sorry, please continue.

1: At one time I had even said that if heaven was like that I didn't want to go!

2: Oh?

1: Too restricting, too routine . . . excuse me, too

14

boring! An eternity of white robes and the "Halleluia Chorus" was hardly my idea of fun!

2: Heaven was to be a place for fun, eh?

1: Oh, I suppose I could use some nice, fancy, very spiritual words, but I would really have meant "fun"!

2: What about . . . "fulfillment"?

1: A little too fancy for me. But in my dream, it didn't matter . . . it really didn't.

2: The dream made you feel real good, eh?

1: HEAVEN made me feel real good.

2: I see.

1: I hope so.

2: So you're no longer concerned whether or not your dream about death is ominous?

1: That's right. I was dead, yes, but never more fully alive!

2: Well, what do you know?

1: THAT'S . . . what I know!

5.

. . . I Was a Very, Very Famous Theologian

1: The other night I dreamed I was a very, very famous theologian.

2: Oh?

1: So famous that all of my books—and I had written hundreds—had been translated into every known language, living and dead!

2: I see.

1: And all of my works were quoted by other famous theologians, copied by would-be-theologians and memorized by seminarians and junior confirmands.

2: Not many men attain such lofty heights.

1: I was considered the last word in any and every theological debate, however heated and labyrinthine the argument.

2: You were the final word, eh?

1: Inveterate heresy-hunters couldn't fault me, try as they might, nor could the avant-garde label me "dated."

2: Beyond reproach, eh?

1: Everyone suggested—indeed, some held it as an article of faith—that my works provided both the axis and the dynamic for the ecumenical movement.

2: That must have been quite a movement.

1: I was also loved, even revered, by the humble lay-folk.

2: A man for all vocations, eh?

1: I was able to express the most profound thoughts with childlike simplicity . . .

2: A rare gift, indeed.

1: . . . and I was a master at using just the right touch of bawdy humor.

2: At home in both nursery and pub, eh?

1: In my free time, among other things, I advised leading nuclear physicists and judged World Master Chess Tournaments.

2: One might have suspected that.

1: I also coached a little league baseball team.

2: Each season a winning season, eh?

1: Our lads were, to a man, gracious winners.

2: Your example, no doubt.

1: No doubt.

2: And you had a dog?

1: A tri-champion: field, obedience, and bench!

2: No!

1: Best-in-Show, Westminster.

2: It would have to have been Westminster, wouldn't it?

1: I also, through sheer discipline, found time to serve as a consulting editor for *Playboy*, *Ms.*, and *Popular Mechanics*.

2: Really?

1: And one year I was voted Husband, Father, Son, Friend, Man, and Person of the . . .

2: Year?

1: Decade!

2: Almost Unbelievable!

1: I kept the trophies, plaques, and scrolls but gave all monies—which were considerable—to charity.

2: I . . . I just don't know what to say.

1: One day—and this is where my dream really becomes significant—one day a chariot came down from heaven! I was working, at the time, on a pollution-control project, next to the brewery. Yes, I was whisked away to the Golden Stairway.

2: I don't know if I can stand any more!

1: Trumpets, a thousand strong, sounded as I walked up to the Mother-of-Pearl Gates!

18

2: Please, I . . .

1: The gates opened . . .

2: And?

1: . . . someone gave me an enormous . . . KICK IN THE PANTS!

2: Halleluia!

1: I woke up . . . in excruciating pain!

2: Good!

1: I had fallen out of bed . . .

2: Oh?

1: . . . nearly fracturing my pelvis on my bowling ball, which had rolled out from under my bed!

2: Divine judgment, agreed?

1: Divine mercy!

2: Mercy?

1: Indeed!

2: Oh?

1: I had only been cast out of BED!

6.

... I Was a Pamphylian

1: Not too long ago I dreamed I was a Pamphylian.

2: A what?

1: A Pamphylian ... from Pamphylia.

2: Oh?

1: You don't hear much about Pamphylia today, do you?

2: No, I guess you don't.

1: But there I was ... a Pamphylian.

2: Puzzling, eh?

1: Only because I was talking to a Phrygian.

2: You were what?

1: That's right, I was talking to a Phrygian.

2: A Phrygian what?

1: Just a plain, old Phrygian.

2: I see.

1: And I didn't know a single word of Phrygian!

2: Not one Phrygian word, eh?

1: But he understood me and I understood him!

2: Mutual understanding is always a kind of miracle, isn't it?

1: I told you about the tongues of fire, did I?

2: The what?

1: Tongues of fire. Little, lapping tongues of fire. And wind ... a whirling, churning wind.

2: Fire?

1: And wind . . . like a bunch of wee, little tornadoes.

2: Puzzling, eh?

1: Not to me and this Phrygian.

2: Oh?

1: The fire and wind were just sort of in the background.

2: Not all that important, eh?

1: Not unimportant, mind you, just . . .

2: Just?

1: . . . not in the foreground.

2: And what WAS in the foreground?

1: Me and the Phrygian!

2: You two were the focus of attention?

1: That's right.

2: More important than that miraculous display of . . . miracles?

1: Man, we were the miracles!

2: Oh?

1: Don't you realize that that was the first time in recorded history that a Pamphylian ever spoke to a Phrygian?

2: I guess I didn't know that.

1: Prior to this happening all we ever did was laugh at one another . . . laugh, laugh, laugh, laugh, laugh!

2: Rebuke is laughter-gone-wild.

1: You should have heard some of the Phrygie jokes we used to tell.

2: Cruel, eh?

1: But there we were . . . talking!

21

2: And you felt good, eh?

1: I felt great!

2: Simple conversation can be exhilarating, not to say intoxicating, can't it?

1: Simple conversation?

2: You know . . . idle chitchat.

1: Phrygians don't chit . . .

2: Oh?

1: And Pamphylians don't . . .

2: Chat?

1: We were talking about God!

2: God?

1: That's right.

2: The first words you spoke were about God?

1: Yes.

2: Puzzling, eh?

1: On the contrary!

2: What?

1: We solved the puzzle.

2: Oh?

1: Absolutely!

2: So?

1: When a Phrygian and a Pamphylian discover that they love and are loved by the same God . . .

2: Yes?

1: Watch out!

7.

. . . I Was About Twelve Years Old

1: The other night I dreamed that I was about twelve years old and that I was standing in a temple talking with learned, pious, old men.

2: In a temple, eh?

1: I was, in fact, the center of attention.

2: It's always nice to be noticed, isn't it?

1: I was asking such profound questions that even the most learned among them could only shake his head in disbelief and wonder.

2: You really impressed them, eh?

1: If the truth were known, I was frightened, really frightened, by the power of my questions.

2: Power is in many ways a frightening reality, isn't it?

1: Then they began asking me questions.

2: Oh?

1: Question after question after question.

2: That's only fair, isn't it?

1: They asked me many of the same questions that I had asked them!

2: The ones they couldn't answer?

1: And do you know what?

2: What?

1: Would you believe it?

2: Believe what?

1: I couldn't answer any of them!

2: What?

1: Not one!

2: No!

1: Absolutely stumped!

2: Embarrassing, eh?

1: Not in the least!

2: You weren't?

1: The eldest of them simply smiled, patted my shoulder and said, oh, so very gently, "That's all right, my son, don't worry. You are not the one."

2: Not the one?

1: "You are not the one."

2: Now, that must have been embarrassing, wasn't it?

1: Of course not.

2: It wasn't?

1: I was relieved to learn that I wasn't the one.

2: Relieved?

1: Who wants to answer questions when you can ask them?

8.

. . . I Was an Old, Old Man

1: The other night I dreamed that I was an old, old man.

2: Oh?

1: Isn't it kind of strange that I who am young, strong, virile—at the very height of my creative and procreative powers—would dream that I was old?

2: It would appear that people have always been preoccupied with growing old.

1: Does that mean that we're afraid of old age?

2: That could be one interpretation of the phenomenon.

1: But is it the "right" interpretation?

2: No single interpretation is the "right interpretation.

1: What does that mean?

2: Simply that no single interpretation can explain why everyone who dreams the dream dreams it.

1: And what does that mean?

2: It's a puzzling dream, isn't it?

1: This one was really puzzling. I'm anxious to see what you make of it.

2: Of course, it's more important to see what you make of it.

1: You always say that. Aren't you the least bit curious about what my dreams mean?

2: Please continue.

1: I don't want to bore you.

2: Boredom is always unpleasant, isn't it?

1: Then I'm not boring you?

2: I'd like to hear about this dream.

1: OK. I dreamed that I was old and . . . poor! Very, very poor! Now, wait a minute, I bet you're going to tell me that people have always been preoccupied with becoming poor, right?

2: Is that one of your preoccupations?

1: I don't think so. You see, I had a paper route as a kid . . . plus a good allowance. And, no, I was definitely not a depression baby!

2: Solvent throughout your formative years, eh?

1: I suppose so, anyway, in this dream I was poor and . . . sick.

2: Old, poor, and sick, eh?

1: And a beggar!

2: A poor, old, sick beggar.

1: That's right. What do you make out of it so far?

2: What you make out of it is more important.

1: There you go again. You know, it just may be . . .

2: Yes?

1: It just may be that you have a really low image of yourself.

2: What?

1: You're always putting yourself down, as though what you thought didn't count for anything or that your ideas weren't worth listening to.

2: Oh?

1: You are as important as I am . . . your preoccupations are as important as mine . . . your fears are as valid as mine!

2: So if I dreamed that I was a poor, old, sick beggar I would have the right to be as fearful as you, right?

1: Right!

2: Shall we talk about those fears?

1: Let me finish the dream first, OK?

2: If you prefer.

1: Each day I dragged myself to the gateway of a rich man's house, a particular rich man. That was my spot, mine alone, off limits to any other beggar . . . and the city was crawling with them.

2: But you had this really choice location, eh?

1: It was a lousy location! He never gave me a thing . . . coin or crust! Oh, yes, he did give me something: advice!

2: Oh?

1: He forever quoted the Bible.

2: Yes?

1: From Monday to Friday it was always, "Consider the ant, thou sluggard!" And on weekends: "A fool and his money are soon parted!"

2: But you still kept coming back to that same spot and that same abuse day after day after day?

1: I know it sounds kind of sick . . . but sick like a fox!

2: Oh?

1: You see, I knew I was dying and I wanted to die there, right there, right on his front doorstep.

2: Oh?

1: "Let my death be on his conscience!" . . . that selfish, miserable, miserly murderer!

2: You were a kind of moral visual aid, eh?

27

1: I suppose so, but now we get to the part of the dream that is very symbolic . . . or something like that. At least, it's kind of hard to believe.

2: OK.

1: I finally died . . . and went to heaven.

2: I see.

1: And a couple of days later the rich guy dies and goes right straight to hell.

2: One might have suspected that.

1: But one wouldn't have suspected what followed.

2: Oh?

1: I could see him in hell and he could see me in heaven. In some strange way we were even able to carry on a conversation.

2: I wouldn't have suspected that.

1: I told you that this was a very symbolic dream. Anyway, there he was in hell suffering, I mean he was really suffering . . . fire and poisonous gases all over the place . . . it was just plain . . . well, let me put it this way: a sick, twisted, perverted mind couldn't have devised worse punishment! It made the Inquisition look like a chapter from *Winnie the Pooh*!

2: I see.

1: Whereas I, in heaven, was lounging by a deep, cool, crystal-clear pool, the water lightly scented with jasmine petals. I was drinking a tall frosty glass of something that tasted like a mixture of pomegranate juice and tonic water. And throughout the day, the rich guy was screaming for water, a drop of water, a breath of water. . . . "Please," he screamed and choked and coughed, "just dip your finger in the cool water and touch my lips!" Man you should have heard him scream!

2: That must surely have ruined your otherwise idyllic existence.

1: On the contrary, it made it!

2: It what?

1: He had watched me suffer for, lo, my four-score-and-ten . . . but now I could watch him suffer throughout eternity!

2: And that . . . excuse me, but that gave you pleasure?

1: You'd better believe it did!

2: And you were in heaven?

1: Of course, I was!

2: Rejoicing over the suffering of a fellow human being?

1: Well . . .

2: Well?

1: Well, you know what it says.

2: What does it say?

1: Do unto others . . . as they have done unto you.

2: Where does it say that?

1: Well . . .

2: Well?

1: I just thought of something.

2: Yes?

1: It may be that heaven is a lot like the church.

2: Oh?

1: It's easier to be *in* it than *of* it!

9.

. . . I Was on the Johnny Carson Show

1: The other night I dreamed that I was on the Johnny Carson Show.

2: Oh?

1: Together with a world-renowned psychiatrist.

2: Oh?

1: Believe it or not, he looked a good deal like you.

2: Oh?

1: A little younger, of course . . . and thinner.

2: Who isn't?

1: You'll probably never guess what we were discussing.

2: Probably not.

1: Prayer!

2: Prayer?

1: That's right . . . the pro's and con's of prayer.

2: I see.

1: Guess which side I was on.

2: No middle ground, eh?

1: In something as important as prayer, there is no middle ground!

2: I see.

1: I was FOR prayer!

2: On the side of the angels, so to speak.

1: Angels? I believe in prayer not in angels . . . necessarily.

2: Oh?

1: You even sound like the guy in my dream.

2: I do?

1: And I'll bet that you don't believe in prayer.

2: But, of course, if prayer has such great meaning for you, then what I believe is of little consequence, right?

1: To me, no, but what about to you?

2: You consider prayer to be of supreme importance in a person's life, right?

1: Absolutely.

2: But the fellow on the T.V. show disagreed, eh?

1: He said—among other things—that prayer was an attempt to escape from personal choices and responsibilities.

2: Oh?

1: "Let God do it" and all that kind of stuff.

2: I see.

1: I'm afraid I became rather angry at times.

2: Oh?

1: More than once Johnny had to cut in with a commercial even though one wasn't scheduled.

2: You felt that strongly on the matter, eh?

1: At one point he said that prayer was little other than . . . autosuggestion.

2: Oh?

1: That means "talking yourself into doing or believing something."

2: Really?

1: Which means that prayer is not, in fact, an otherworldly kind of miracle at all.

2: I see.

31

1: It means that prayer is a way of drawing upon one's "inner resources."

2: Oh?

1: That means inner strength . . . like courage, patience . . . well, you get the idea.

2: Of course.

1: It's not too bad an argument.

2: You found yourself agreeing with him?

1: Well, not exactly . . . I mean . . . well . . .

2: It would have bothered you to have agreed with him?

1: Well I can imagine that sometimes—but only once in a while—I am really . . . just . . . sort of . . . talking to myself.

2: To yourself?

1: Yes.

2: No miracle then?

1: It's more of a . . . mystery.

2: Oh?

1: On those occasions I may be talking to myself, true, but . . .

2: But?

1: I'm absolutely convinced that . . .

2: Yes?

1: . . . that Someone else is listening!

10.

. . . I Was Awakened by Five Screaming Women

1: You absolutely will not believe what I dreamed last night.

2: Quite a dream, eh?

1: Absolutely unbelievable! I dreamed that it was a little after midnight and that I was at home, in my bedroom, fast asleep!

2: That's unbelievable?

1: Suddenly there was this frantic knocking, pounding, beating, writhing at the front door!

2: Oh?

1: I put on my pajamas, lit a candle, and stumbled my way down the stairway to the front door.

2: Still pretty believable, if you ask me.

1: I heard sobbing and crying and wailing coming from outside the door. I opened it . . . and guess what was there?

2: You tell me.

1: No, come on now . . . guess!

2: You like to have people guess about answers which you already know, right?

1: Right! Now, when I opened the door . . . who was standing there?

2: A woman!

1: No! Not *a* woman!

2: Oh?

1: Five women! Five of them! FIVE!

2: Well, weren't you the lucky one.

1: Five crying, pleading, imploring, desperate women . . . YOUNG women!

2: I would have guessed that.

1: So, OK, guess what they wanted!

2: No, thank you.

1: Come on, try it, you've been right about everything else . . . just about.

2: They wanted . . . YOU!

1: Right! But why did they want me?

2: Because you . . . have such a magnificent body!

1: Thank you, but that's not why they wanted me.

2: Oh?

1: They wanted my oil!

2: What?

1: OIL!

2: Your oil?

1: Yes! Oh, I forgot to tell you, I was an oil merchant. The only one in the city.

2: Unbelievable, absolutely unbelievable!

1: That's NOT the unbelievable part!

2: No?

1: Why do you think they wanted the oil?

2: Because they had run out of oil.

1: Yes, but WHY had they run out?

2: You tell me.

1: They had been waiting all night for the arrival of the Bridegroom. He was supposed to arrive at eight o'clock, but, no. Nine o'clock, ten, ten-thirty, eleven . . . no Bridegroom. At eleven-forty-five . . . no oil, no oil no light.

2: Now that is unbelievable!

1: No it's not! The unbelievable part is that five of their friends, friends who were waiting for the Bridegroom with them, HAD oil! But they wouldn't share it with them!

2: No?

1: I told you you wouldn't believe this dream!

2: Incredible!

1: The selfish five were afraid that they, too, would run out of oil before the Bridegroom arrived.

2: That must have been a pretty important event for them . . .

1: Of course it was!

2: . . . one that required particular and unusual preparation.

1: Of course it did!

2: Then why do you fault them for protecting themselves from their less-careful friends?

1: I fault them because in the midst of waiting for the big, important event they forgot something as big and as important!

2: Oh?

1: That they were still their sisters' keepers!

11.

. . . I Was, of All Things, a Sheep

1: If a person dreams that he's not himself, is that bad?

2: Dreams, in and of themselves, are neither good nor bad.

1: Yes, but if you dream that you're not yourself but something else, is that bad?

2: You dreamed that you were someone other than yourself?

1: Not someone . . . something!

2: Oh?

1: I dreamed that I was, of all things, a sheep!

2: A sheep.

1: Now is that or isn't that bad?

2: You're afraid that it is bad?

1: Not afraid exactly, but . . . at least, concerned!

2: Oh?

1: And not because it's bad . . . just unusual.

2: So it's unusual.

1: I thought so. I wonder what it means when a person dreams he's some sort of animal? And why was I a sheep? Why wasn't I a lion or a panther . . . or a racehorse?

2: Sheep aren't too appealing, eh?

1: I could have been an elk . . . or a Doberman Pinscher! But, no, I was a sheep!

2: Tell me about the dream.

1: Well, I was one of about a hundred sheep that belonged to this particular shepherd.

2: Yes?

1: One-hundred-to-one is not a very good sheep-shepherd ratio! No school board would allow it.

2: And you didn't like it either, eh?

1: I guess I didn't. Mind you, I wasn't picked on any more than the other sheep and I wasn't ignored any more than the rest, it's just that I had my doubts.

2: Doubts?

1: That the shepherd really knew me . . . really cared for me.

2: Sheep or not, those are important concerns.

1: So I decided to do something about it.

2: Oh?

1: I decided to pretend that I was lost!

2: Yes?

1: Just pretend, mind you, since that's about all the courage a sheep has!

2: The prospect of being REALLY lost didn't appeal to you, eh?

1: Not at all! When you get right down to it, I'd rather be ignored but safe than be looked for but lost! You know, I may have looked like a sheep but I certainly thought like a person!

2: So?

1: That very night I stealthily strayed from the flock and hid just over a little ridge.

2: And?

1: The next day I stayed behind that ridge and just

peeked over occasionally to check on things. I wish I hadn't!

2: Oh?

1: My worst fears were confirmed!

2: Oh?

1: I wasn't even missed!

2: No one was calling your name?

1: That's sad, isn't it? Someone should write a song about that: "No One Was Calling My Name!"

2: Yes, that's very sad!

1: Well, don't take it too hard . . . things improved!

2: Improved?

1: I spent the entire next week, day and night, hiding from the flock . . . and still no one missed me, shepherd or sheep!

2: That was an improvement?

1: Just wait a minute, don't rush me. Finally, I got so angry that I ran back to the flock, flew through the ewes, right up to the shepherd!

2: Well, that was courageous enough.

1: I don't know if you know how a sheep looks when he's angry, but I looked that way! My wool stood on end! I looked like an electrified brillo pad!

2: That angry, eh?

1: But the shepherd just turned to me . . . get this
. . . he just turned to me and smiled! SMILED!

2: What do you know about that?

1: And then he did the most beautiful thing.

2: Yes?

1: He called me by my first name and asked if I had
enjoyed my little game! Imagine that! He DID
know my name! And he WAS watching over me!
He saw me sneaking away that first night . . . up
over the ridge . . . spying on them from behind all
those rocks and bushes! I wasn't out of his sight all
week!

2: He knew you were pretending all along, eh?

1: Absolutely!

2: And it didn't bother you that he didn't play along
with you and pretend to be looking for you?

1: Oh, no! It would have really bothered me if he
had!

2: Oh?

1: It's good to know that when you're comparing
sheep and shepherd . . .

2: Yes?

1: Only sheep pretend!

12.

. . . I Was Eating with the Pigs

1: This past week I had a dream that very nearly turned my stomach!

2: Oh?

1: It was absolutely sickening! I'm not even sure that I want to talk about it.

2: Whatever you wish.

1: It was disgusting. Revolting! I just don't want to say anything more.

2: Fine.

1: Do you want to hear about it or don't you?

2: Only if you want to tell me.

1: I'm afraid that I might . . . vomit. It was that bad.

2: Then let's not talk about it.

1: You don't want to hear about my dream?

2: Tell me the dream.

1: I was sitting in this . . . barnyard.

2: Yes?

1: I was sitting in this barnyard . . . eating.

2: Eating?

1: I was sitting in this barnyard eating . . . WITH THE PIGS!

2: Oh.

1: "Oh"? Is that all you're going to say? I said I was eating with dirty, filthy, smelly PIGS!

2: I see.

1: Well, aren't you going to ask me WHY I was eating with the pigs?

2: Why were you eating with the pigs?

1: I was starving! There was nothing else to eat . . . nowhere else to go . . . no one invited me home for dinner or lunch or breakfast . . . not even for a peanut butter sandwich!

2: All alone, eh?

1: Except for the pigs. And—to make matters worse —they didn't like me!

2: Oh?

1: One great, big, old, fat, slobbering pig kept look-

ing at me . . . grunted and looked, looked and grunted . . . and finally said, "You're not one of us. Go home!"

2: Quite a put-down, eh?

1: That's what I thought, at first. But then it struck me like a bolt of lightning! The pig was right! I didn't belong there!

2: So?

1: Ah, then I woke up.

2: Oh.

1: I tried to fall asleep again in order to finish the dream. Did I go home again or didn't I? Did I even have a home to go to? If I did, what was that home like and why did I leave?

2: And?

1: No luck. Only God knows how that dream might have ended.

2: Oh?

1: But as I lay there trying to go to sleep again, the strangest thought kept running through my mind. Really bizarre!

2: Oh?

1: But . . . it's too embarrassing to talk about . . . too stupid.

2: OK.

1: People wouldn't understand . . . they'd think I was crazy.

2: OK.

1: I got to wondering . . . how many other young guys may have started the long journey homeward because some pig told them, "You don't belong here, sonny, go home!"?

13.

. . . I Started Homeward

1: I did it! Again! For the second time!

2: Oh?

1: I don't know how I did it but I did it!

2: Yes?

1: The second chapter for a dream I told you about some time ago!

2: The second chapter, eh?

1: The one about the pigs . . . where I was starving, remember?

2: Oh, yes, where you received such good counsel from one of your snouted dinner companions, right?

1: Well, in this second chapter I took his advice—I started home!

2: Really.

1: Oh, to begin with I did a great deal of aimless wandering because, frankly, I didn't know which way to go, but the important thing was that I began!

2: That took some courage, didn't it?

1: Things, little things, began to click . . . slowly, very slowly . . . so I started walking north . . . north along an old goat trail.

2: Goat trail?

1: Goat trail, camel trail, I don't know which, but it didn't matter.

2: You were on your way home, eh?

1: Maybe I'm part homing pigeon, I don't know, but I just felt that I was going in the right direction.

2: That must have been exciting.

1: It was, believe me, it was! After several weeks of continuous walking, I got out of the desert and entered a region that turned out to be a lush, green valley.

2: You were still on the right track, eh?

1: I was so sure I was that I did a kind of . . . ceremonial thing.

2: Ceremonial?

1: I took a bath!

2: Well, what do you know?

1: In a gentle, little crystal-clear stream. And I washed my clothes . . . or what was left of them . . . combed my hair and beard as best I could, yes, I had a beard, scruffy though it was. I even brushed my teeth . . . with a juniper twig, I think.

2: So you washed away the reminders of your old life, eh?

1: I was still terribly hungry, terribly hungry, but, surprisingly, I felt no pain, none whatsoever!

2: Maybe the juniper bush was really peyote.

1: Peyote? In the Holy Land? Of course not! It was juniper, I know it was!

2: Could it have been the prospect of getting home that gave you your sense of well-being?

1: I soon came to some small, sharecropper shacks, but you know what?

2: What?

1: I knew, I just knew I didn't belong there!

2: Oh?

1: Something told me that I belonged . . . well, that I belonged to better things.

2: Born to the purple, eh?

1: I walked by some bigger and fancier places, but even these weren't home.

2: Just not "you," eh?

1: Finally, I came to the ritzy section . . . huge fields, magnificent villas. And there, something told me —I don't know what to call it, call it what you will —something told me I was home!

2: Exciting, eh?

1: I was in sort of a trance. As if under a spell I began walking toward one particular villa, the most magnificent in the area. I walked slowly down the lane, my heart beating like a drum, little rivulets of tears starting down my cheeks, and then . . .

2: Yes?

1: A young fellow, about my age, came riding up on a big white stallion. I saw him in the distance and I swear I just about . . . swooned!

2: Swooned?

1: A word welled up in my stomach, slowly worked its way up my throat, on to my lips . . .

2: Yes?

1: Brother! ! ! Maybe this . . . was . . . my brother! I began to wave, to shout . . . and then . . .

2: Yes?

1: He just about rode me down with his horse!

2: He did what?

45

1: Yes! He charged me on that huge beast! And he shouted at me, hatred propelling every word!

2: Yes?

1: "Where do you think you're going?" I tried to regain my composure. Perhaps I'd been away so long that he'd forgotten me. I grant you, I didn't look as though I belonged anywhere but with the pigs! Then I said as inoffensively as I could, "This is my home, I think."

2: And?

1: He laughed a maniacal laugh and screamed, "You've got to be dreaming!"

2: And then?

1: Wouldn't you know it, wouldn't you just know it?

2: What?

1: I WOKE UP!

2: No.

1: Wide awake, sitting bolt upright in bed, sweating like a horse!

2: End of chapter two, eh?

1: And I still wasn't quite home!

2: Well, the fellow on the horse was right about one thing.

1: What?

2: You were dreaming.

1: Yes, but what kind of brother would ruin another brother's dream?

14.

. . . I Found My Brother and Wished I Hadn't

1: Do you believe in miracles?

2: In miracles?

1: What I'm going to tell you will absolutely blow your mind!

2: That incredible, eh?

1: And it's going to make you world famous!

2: Say, that's a bit of all right!

1: You can write this up for *Psychology Today*! It may even make *Reader's Digest*!

2: It's that important, eh?

1: With a little luck it might earn you a Nobel prize!

2: Well, let's begin. What's behind this flight into fame?

1: I have just dreamed the third chapter, the third chapter, in my life among the pigs and my encounter with my "loving" brother!

2: That one again?

1: This is a "first," isn't it? I mean, have you ever read of anyone else dreaming dreams a chapter at a time? The way things are going, this dream could become a major novel . . . maybe even a T.V. series!

2: This thematic development is at least interesting.

1: Just interesting?

2: Oh, no, more than interesting. It's undoubtedly an earth-shaking experience for you, and why not?

1: But it's no big deal for you, eh?

2: It's more important that the dream has meaning for you.

1: Well, let me tell you, this one has meaning for me!

2: Good.

1: The fellow on the white horse, you remember, the one who tried to trample me to death, the one who told me that I was dreaming?

2: Yes?

1: Turns out he WAS my brother!

2: Oh?

1: Brother, what a brother! He must have taken lessons from Cain!

2: That cruel, eh?

1: I was knocked to the ground, somewhat stunned, but I could still see the horse rearing over me . . . ready to give me the ol' coup de grace . . . BUT THEN . . .

2: You woke up?

1: Then the most beautiful thing happened!

2: Yes?

1: I heard trumpets playing some sort of "Here Comes the Chief" music, and down the lane came this huge golden chariot . . .

2: Golden chariot?

1: . . . pulled by four white horses. At the sound of the trumpet and the sight of the chariot, my brother, bless him, took off in the opposite direction!

2: Rescued, were you?

1: The chariot roared to a halt and out jumped an

old man who ran over to me, looked at me, and then knelt beside me crying, "My son, my son, you've come home!"

2: A very touching scene.

1: You'd better believe it! But then . . .

2: NOW you woke up?

1: Not yet.

2: That's a relief. The suspense is killing me!

1: I told you that this would make a good T.V. series! Anyway, when I came to, I was lying in this huge bed, in a huge room, attended by a huge servant.

2: Everything huge, eh?

1: When the servant saw that I was awake, he hurried out of the room and quickly returned with my father or, at least, with the man who called me his son, which, I suppose, made him my father.

2: You still didn't know for sure, eh?

1: I must have been away from home for a long time, a very long time and . . . and really have done some hairy things . . . things that I was so anxious to forget that I forgot him, too! I guess I forgot the good along with the bad. Does that make sense?

2: It's certainly possible.

1: But why is it possible for the bad to be so bad that you forget the good? Why couldn't the good be so good that you forget the bad?

2: Does it have to be one way or the other?

1: Well, let me tell you . . . I had a mighty tough time remembering the good that he was talking about. And he talked for days and days, describing a "me" that I would really like to have been . . . or, for that matter, become. Oh, well . . .

2: Know what?

1: What?

2: I have the uneasy feeling that you're going to tell me that the dream ended there. Right?

1: Right. But this time it was different. I woke up . . . at peace with myself . . . breathing slowly and deeply . . . smiling . . . a Mona Lisa smile.

2: Even though your questions were not all answered?

1: Enough of them had been answered. Anyway . . .

2: Yes?

1: . . . with a father like that . . .

2: Yes?

1: . . . who worries about incidentals!

15.

. . . I Was God

1: I woke up this morning and for a fleeting moment thought that I was God.

2: Thought you were God, eh?

1: But the longer I was awake the less convinced I was about it.

2: The thought slowly vanished, eh?

1: So . . .

2: So?

1: I went back to bed!

2: Where you were God once again, eh?

1: But I had the strangest dream!

2: Strange, eh?

1: I dreamed that I died!

2: Died, eh?

1: I, God, died!

2: That must have been philosophically unsettling.

1: UNSETTLING? ? ? Man, I was CRUCIFIED! ! !

2: Psychologically wrenched, eh?

1: I'M TALKING ABOUT HAMMERS AND NAILS AND . . . AND A SPEAR! ! !

2: Did you say "a spear"?

1: Here and here and there and there and HERE!

2: The spear got you where?

1: Here!

2: There?

1: Right here!

2: And then?

1: I died.

2: Oh?

1: Died.

2: And then?

1: I woke up.

2: Oh?

1: But I learned something.

2: Yes?

1: At least, I think I learned something.

2: It's good to learn from one's experiences, isn't it?

1: I learned . . .

2: You learned?

1: I think I learned . . .

2: Something about "resurrection"?

1: I learned that I'd rather be me than God!

16.

. . . I Was Standing Before
a Great Body of Water

1: I once imagined myself standing before a great body of water.

2: Water, eh?

1: It wasn't a river. It was a sea . . . wide and deep.

2: Liked to fish as a kid, eh?

1: Couldn't stand it.

2: Oh?

1: The worms.

2: Didn't like to touch them, eh?

1: Didn't like to kill them.

2: Oh.

1: But there I was . . . standing by this sea . . . wide and deep.

2: Wide and deep, eh?

1: Wide and deep.

2: I liked to skip rocks when I was a kid.

1: I didn't.

2: Oh?

1: They'd hit the water once and then . . . glug, glug, glug.

2: The sea can be cruel and lonely, can't it?

1: I wasn't lonely.

2: Oh?

1: Thousands of people were with me.

2: That's a few people.

1: And they all knew me.

2: They all knew you, eh?

1: By my first and last names.

2: No wonder you weren't lonely.

1: But I didn't know them! They knew me . . . first name, last name . . . but I didn't know them.

2: That must have been a funny feeling.

1: What they wanted me to do was even funnier.

2: Oh?

1: You wouldn't believe what they wanted me to do!

2: That strange, eh?

1: They wanted me to . . .

2: Yes?

1: To save them.

2: To do what?

1: To save them.

2: Oh?

1: From destruction.

2: Destruction?

1: Destruction.

2: They were going to be destroyed, eh?

1: Within the hour.

2: I wouldn't have wanted to have been in your shoes.

1: I didn't want to be in my shoes!

2: So?

1: I took them off and threw them away.

2: And?

1: Another guy took over . . . led the mob right, smack, dab THROUGH that wide, deep sea.

2: And . . . and what happened to you?

1: I followed along at the tail end, at the very tail end . . . barefoot and alone.

2: Swallowed your pride, eh?

1: Better that than a ton of sea water!

17.

. . . I Was Adam

1: The other night I dreamed that I was Adam.

2: Adam?

1: Yes, Adam . . . in the Garden of Eden . . . alone and naked.

2: You were naked, eh?

1: Adam was naked, I was Adam, I was naked—yes, I was naked.

2: And that bothered you?

1: No, it didn't bother me.

2: That's good. It shouldn't.

1: It didn't.

2: Good.

1: But if it had bothered me, why would that be so bad?

2: It wouldn't.

1: It wouldn't?

2: No.

1: Then why was it so good that it didn't bother me in the first place?

2: You dreamed you were in the Garden of Eden, eh?

1: I suppose so.

2: Suppose?

1: Well, where else would Adam live?

2: The analytical mind is a fascinating phenomenon, isn't it?

1: There I was in the Garden . . . and you know what?

2: What?

1: I was NOT lonely!

2: Not lonely, eh?

1: Incredible, isn't it?

2: You thought it incredible, did you?

1: At least, significant . . . VERY significant.

2: That you weren't lonely?

1: I was simply too busy!

2: Busy, were you?

1: Day and night!

2: Why do you think you were so busy?

1: Think? I KNOW why I was so busy!

2: You do?

1: Paradise didn't just happen! It took work, believe me, it took WORK!

2: I believe you.

1: Look at these blisters and calluses! And remember that I was just dreaming!

2: That bothers you?

1: What bothers me?

2: That.

1: It wasn't the work that bothered me.

2: That's good.

1: Good, bad, bothered, wasn't bothered, that's all beside the point!

2: What, then, is the point?

1: I wasn't lonely! Believe me, I was NOT lonely!

2: I believe you.

1: I don't care if you do or don't believe me, I wasn't lonely!

2: I believe that you were not lonely.

1: Too many things to do . . . too many animals to take care of, for one thing. Say, did you know that the aardvark was Adam's best friend?

2: The aardvark, you say?

1: I was NOT lonely . . . and that . . . that's my problem.

2: Problem?

1: Not to be lonely is to be less than Adam!

2: And that bothers you?

1: THAT . . . bothers me!

18.

. . . I Had Been Reading the Bible

1: I had a really horrible dream the other night and for once I know, I really know, why I had it.

2: Oh?

1: I had been reading the Bible.

2: Reading the Bible gives you horrible dreams?

1: That night it did! I don't know why they leave stuff like that in the Bible. It's worse, much worse, than hard-core pornography!

2: Very out of place, eh?

1: It was sick! No purpose to it . . . just plain cruel . . . totally, absolutely senseless!

2: The only senseless part of the Bible?

1: Well, I can't say that for sure.

2: Oh?

1: I tell people that I've read the Good Book from cover to cover but I haven't. Frankly, the plot gets a little weak at times . . . too much geography . . . too much history . . . and all those strange names, worse than a Russian novel!

2: I see.

1: But I surely hope that there are no other parts as senseless as the part that forced me to have such a terrifying dream!

2: "Forced me to have such a terrifying dream" . . . what does that mean?

1: I'll bet a million dollars that anyone and everyone

who reads that part has a terrifying dream! That's why it doesn't belong in the Bible. It's about time that someone had the guts to take it out.

2: Tell me about it.

1: The Bible story?

2: Your dream.

1: I'd rather talk about my views of the Bible.

2: I'm afraid that wouldn't be of much help just now.

1: But you will admit that the Bible creates certain problems for a critical reader?

2: By critical you mean . . . serious and informed?

1: Of course!

2: Tell me about the dream.

1: OK, but remember, I didn't just dream this. It's a factual recounting of a story from the Bible, the story about a prophet, of all things! And I'm not making it up!

2: I'm sure you aren't.

1: I want to make it perfectly clear that it's not ME that's sick! It's the . . . well, I don't want to go quite THAT far!

2: Please, the dream?

1: Well, OK. I was a small boy playing with a bunch of other small boys. You know what it's like when small boys get together. Nothing really bad happens, but . . . well . . .

2: Boys will be boys, eh?

1: Imagine what forty or so Tom Sawyers and Huckleberry Finns would be like. Maybe a little noisy but certainly not destructive or violent. Sure, tease the girls a little . . . sneak the occasional cigarette

61

. . . steal a couple of green apples . . . but nothing serious!

2: Who would miss a couple dozen green apples?

1: Remember, now, this was hundreds and hundreds of years ago, way back in Bible times. Anyway, we were playing outside the village, you know, just playing. Anyway, this old man comes walking down the road. And we, in all innocence, of course, began teasing him. Don't ask me why, we just began teasing him.

2: Just teasing, eh?

1: Cross my heart, just teasing . . . no sticks or stones . . . we didn't throw a thing. All we said was, "Go up, you baldhead! Go up, you baldhead!" He was bald, you see . . . just a little fringe around the side. Now, tell me, was that so bad?

2: Was ridiculing his baldness bad, is that the question?

1: Well, we could have ridiculed his nose . . . man, what a beak!

2: Wait a minute, didn't you say earlier that this man was a prophet?

1: That's right.

2: And you boys knew that he was a prophet?

1: Of course, we did.

2: And you had the cheek to tease a prophet?

1: Kids, like God, are no respecters of persons!

2: What does that mean?

1: We don't play favorites! Everyone's equal in our sight . . . except for little brothers.

2: And that conviction gave you the right to tease whomever you wished, including a prophet . . . a

holy man? You're right, that's a pretty sick episode
. . . absolutely senseless.

1: That's **NOT** the sick part! Wait'll I tell you what
he did to us! That's the terrifying part!

2: Oh?

1: He turned toward the woods just to the side of the
road and screamed at the top of his voice. And out
of the woods came two of the biggest bears you've
ever seen!

2: Bears?

1: Bears! Two of them! And then he sicced them on
on us!

2: He what?

1: That's right! They came charging into us ripping
and clawing . . .

2: You've got to be . . . no, I guess you're not.

1: You're right, I am **NOT** kidding! Most of my bud-
dies were maimed for life! I escaped only because
I fell to the ground and played dead.

2: You're sure the man was a prophet?

1: Oh, he was a prophet, all right, one of the most
famous.

2: Well, what do you know?

1: Oh, now I know something about prophets.

2: Oh?

1: They may be fearless and courageous and right-
eous and valiant and faithful . . . BUT . . . they are
lacking in the most godly of all virtues!

2: Which is?

1: A sense of humor!

2: God has a sense of humor?

1: You bet he has!

2: Oh?

1: How else could he endure little boys . . . and old
prophets!

19.

...I Was Beguiled by
a Sinister Woman

1: I had the most depressing dream last Tuesday.

2: Oh?

1: It was so depressing that I couldn't get out of bed for two days!

2: That depressing, eh?

1: Missed a basketball game and a physics test.

2: Dreams can be costly, can't they?

1: I was the strongest man in the world.

2: That strong, eh?

1: And I was also the purest man in the world.

2: Quite a combination.

1: I didn't owe my enormous strength to weights or isometrics or Wheaties!

2: Oh?

1: You won't believe what I owed it to!

2: Maybe I won't, but try me.

1: I owed it . . . to my long hair!

2: Well, what do you know about that.

1: Shoulder length . . . with just the slightest natural curl.

2: Another winning combination.

1: But a very sinister person was my undoing.

2: Sinister, eh?

1: Very sinister.

2: And just what did he do to you?

1: He was a she.

2: A what?

1: The sinister person was a she.

2: Oh? The he was a she, eh?

1: The she was a she! Don't worry, I'm not confused about the sexes.

2: You thought I was worried?

1: I know you were worried.

2: Tell me about this sinister person.

1: A woman, she was a woman.

2: OK, tell me about her.

1: I was on the side of Good. She was on the side of Evil.

2: The difference was that obvious, eh?

1: Just as I know the difference between male and female I know the difference between Good and Evil.

2: You're lucky.

1: To make a long story short . . .

2: Yes?

1: . . . she . . .

2: Yes?

1: . . . beguiled me!

2: Beguiled you?

1: Tricked me into telling her the secret of my strength! I told her everything . . . told her about my strength and purity . . . huh, purity? And then . . .

2: Yes?

1: . . . she cut it off!

2: Your hair?

1: What else? I became as weak as a baby. Evil triumphed over Good!

2: That is depressing, isn't it?

1: I was cast into a dungeon, alone. Bald as a baby! Undone by my Achilles-mouth!

2: And that was that, eh?

1: But I learned something.

2: Oh?

1: When it comes to purity and goodness . . .

2: Yes?

1: . . . a blabber-mouth and his hair are soon parted!

20.

. . . *My Hair Grew Back*

1: Did I have a dream last week, I mean, did I have a dream! Man, what a dream!

2: I've never seen you so animated before. Tell me about the dream.

1: Do you remember the dream about my long hair and the sinister woman?

2: Oh, yes, the sinister woman.

1: Well, last night I dreamed the sequel!

2: Oh?

1: Yes! And it was great! I mean, really terrific! Why, the next day I was so high that I scored 38 points in the championship basketball game and wrote an "A" physics test!

2: It must really have turned on the adrenaline!

1: You remember that when the first dream ended I was in a dungeon?

2: Filled with remorse, as I remember.

1: Well, you would be filled with remorse, too, if you'd just been beguiled by a sinister woman!

2: Perhaps so.

1: Particularly if you had been the world's strongest AND purest man!

2: That would certainly aggravate the experience.

1: But guess what happened to me while I was in the dungeon?

2: Something really unusual, eh?

1: No, something very usual, very natural, so natural that I'm surprised I didn't dream it in the first place!

2: That natural, eh?

1: My hair grew back! Longer and more curly than before!

2: But of course!

1: I woke up laughing and shouting for joy! My hair was back! I was the same old me! The sinister woman had been a fool! She should have known that my hair would grow back!

2: What about your virtue . . . your purity?

1: What?

2: Well, didn't you say that you were also the world's purest man?

1: Well, ah . . .

2: The defender of Truth and Goodness?

1: Yes.

2: These things returned with your new, curly locks?

1: Well . . .

2: They weren't a part of this latest dream?

1: Now that you mention it . . . no, they weren't.

2: Oh?

1: You know . . .

2: Yes?

1: . . . I guess it's easier to grow new hair than it is to regrow old virtues!

21.

. . . I Was More Powerful Than a Speeding Locomotive

1: Just recently I've discovered that, among other things, I am more courageous in my dreams than I am in real life.

2: Oh?

1: Nothing frightens me in my dreams, no situation is beyond my control, I am master of whatever Fate deals me!

2: Quite invincible, eh?

1: Only in my dreams. In real life, things are decidedly more chancey, much more iffy!

2: Win a few, lose a few, eh?

1: Win a few, lose a lot! I'm not one of life's big winners, believe me. Of course, I'm not exactly a born loser either, which makes it even worse! I win just enough to know how bitter it is to lose! And I've been top dog just long enough to know the humiliation of being little more than a servant.

2: That would aggravate things.

1: First prize is so sweet that every other prize becomes . . . a dill pickle!

2: A dill pickle?

1: I just made that up. Not bad, eh?

2: Well . . .

1: Never mind, I really want to talk about my dreams and what a hero I am in them.

2: Fine, let's talk about them.

1: OK, but first of all, do you know why—and you may laugh at this—but do you know why I no longer laugh or scoff at what they say about Superman?

2: Superman?

1: You know . . . Clark Kent and Lois Lane?

2: Oh, yes.

1: I no longer laugh because I know what it means to be faster than a bullet, more powerful than a speeding locomotive, able to leap over tall buildings in a single bound . . . in my dreams, of course.

2: You're definitely larger than life, eh?

1: That's putting it mildly. I kid you not, I completely slough off human limitations. In my dreams I actually assume godlike proportions!

2: That's real dreaming.

1: I just thought of something. Isn't it an indictment of the faithlessness of this age that the only time we can become godlike is when we dream?

2: And by godlike you mean strong, victorious, all-powerful, never vanquished . . .

1: All those things . . . and more.

2: You'd like to transfer some of your dream-life into your waking-life, eh?

1: Is that so bad?

2: Is what so bad?

1: To want to live—you know—godlike . . . a winner.

2: Do you think it's bad?

1: Of course not! I'm a Christian!

2: Oh?

1: And I believe that God, in fact, became man.

2: Oh?

1: That he was born, lived, worked and . . .

2: And?

1: Oops!